GW00480715

To my children, Josh, Ellie, Jesse and Fox.
You have been loving and patient teachers to me. I'm sure I have learnt more from you than you from me.

Andy Walker

ME

Hi, thank you for buying this book.

My name is Andy Walker and I have turned 50 this year. I've been a teacher for 30 years, half of which was as a primary school teacher and half as a special needs teacher. I have 4 wonderful children of my own, 2 of which are step children. I have been on multiple courses related to children and completed a large number of children centred courses. I am a practising foster parent.

I'm not writing this to impress you or to let you know that I know it all, because I really don't. Your money has been well spent and however, you're feeling about being a Mum or Dad, this book will, hopefully guide you, reassure you and yes, help you to be a better parent. I don't know all the answers but the mistakes I've made, and I've made a few, actually a lot, if you read this book you won't make them and hopefully you will begin to be slightly more analytical about your parenting.

Being a teacher isn't necessarily that helpful in any way to being a better parent, when you're a teacher you have the power of the schooling system behind you, the power of the headteacher behind you, the power of the school rules behind every request, every command, every look, every comment.

But when you're a parent, you're just this bloke or this woman saying stuff, there is no weight or power behind what you are saying. But it is useful for self-evaluating what you have done. So, this is my special power as it were, every decision, every outcome of those parenting decisions, I have checked, double checked, treble checked and scrutinised, probably every single one. This is what teachers do, when they are at school, trying to find a better way to do something. This is what I have done, when things have been bad, I thought about how you make them good, when they have been good, I have thought about how to make them great and when they have been great, I have thought about how to make them amazing.

So here we are…. Trying to be a better parent.

It will be easier than you think, you're halfway there already, yes really you are half way, maybe further along than you think.

Let's start with a question.

YOU

3

Are you a good parent? Answers anyone? YES...... NO.......

Parenting is ridiculously hard. Single parenting, paired parenting, one child, two children, twins, children with special needs, children in one sense can be utterly charming and beautiful but simultaneously terrifying and frustrating and frightening.

The above question is a stupid one because, especially in this era, it is so so hard. Social media, austerity, schools, bullying, gender roles, you name it, our children have to deal with the whole world of it on their phones and in their bedrooms, that is the WHOLE WORLD all the good stuff and all the bad stuff. I mean the whole world; the internet is great but it is crazy big and it is crazy good and it is crazy bad, and sometimes it can look good but it is bad and sometimes it can look bad, but be good. Plus, hormones, plus big brothers or little sisters, or bad friends. The list goes on and on.

The correct answer to the above question is not YES, but how can that be? What, have you got the answers? BULLSHIT no-one has all the answers partly because your child is different to every other child, but then they are all the same. It is not NO; what are you doing that bad a job - you have just bought this book, that in itself is definitely not a NO. You are not a NO, definitely.

The answer should be I am not sure, or I hope so. I am trying my best is a good answer too, because this is what this book is about. It is not about answers necessarily, although there will be lots of answers, but this is about reflecting on what you (your partner, your husband, your boyfriend) have done and what they (your children) have done and working out how to make it better or easier or happier.

So, the best thing you can be thinking right now is;

Am I doing a good job? Can I do a better job?

How can I do a better job?

Where do I start? You start with the 5 most important things you should be doing with your children.

THEM

Children can be and are really hard work. They can be stubborn and cruel and demanding in a way that very few other things are. They can be relentless, unyielding and just plain mean, BUT in capitals they can be supportive and kind and loyal and loving in ways that I cannot simply put down on paper.

My oldest daughter, at around ten years old, drew a heart in the frosted glass of my car one morning. Just a simple thing like that on a day when I was struggling with my children and my job and it just seemed like it was only to be 'one of those days'; suddenly I am smiling and upbeat and happy. A silly story but true and although that was 25 years ago, it has stayed with me. My oldest children weren't easy when I first arrived on the scene. My oldest son 'ruled the roost' and my oldest daughter was like a feral animal in the wind, doing what she wanted, when she wanted.

It seemed an impossible situation. Obviously, they were not my children at that point, so trying to change what they were and how they were, was really hard. But I managed it. Wow, you say all on your own, well of course not, I needed their help too. Why would they give it to me? if they are running the show and I am probably going to be just another boyfriend and that is all. They helped me, THEY HELPED ME.

They want to be listened to and they want to be loved. They helped me, because fundamentally children want those boundaries and want those rules and need the security of those boundaries and rules. They need all those things. They do not want to be in charge and they do not want to be the boss. They do not want to decide for themselves. Oh, they seem like they do, and any boundaries you set they will push and probe, but really, they are not pushing the boundaries or rules; they are testing you. In 30 years of experience with all kinds of children from special needs children to my own children and most children in between, they all want to be bossed and want to be guided.

That is not to say that all you do is boss them, you do not. You have to respect them and guide them. Guide is a great word to describe what you should be doing for them and with them. Yes, you do give them some choice but never too much choice.

Children are a lot easier to handle than you can imagine.

HOW IT WORKS

This book is about you and your children. It is about you becoming a more reflective parent. It is about you learning new ways of dealing with situations within your home and with you children. It is about being a good role model, and not just having one strategy to deal with a number of different situations and types of children. It is about you and your behaviour having a positive impact on your children. It is about you being aware of the potential impact of how you are and what mood you are in. It is about creating a culture where you can enjoy your children and they can enjoy you. It is divided into 5 parts.

THE FIVE GOLDEN RULES		CONNECTION		ROUTINE		PLAY	
School	P.08	Expectations	P.13	My Time	P.28	Play Theory	P.43
Quality Time	P.09	Behaviour	P.14	Boundaries	P.29	Card Games	P.44
Reading	P.10	Making Mistakes	P.15	Plan Your Day	P.30	Social Media	P.45
Trips	P.11	Consistency	P.16	In The Mornings	P.31	Board Games	P.46
Future Ambitions	P.12	You're In Charge	P.17	Bedtime	P.32	Keep Them Busy	P.47
		Role Model	P.18	Reward Chart	P.33	Getting A Pet	P.48
SPECIAL NEEDS		Are You Listening	P.19	Chores	P.34	Car Journeys	P.49
General	P.55	Positive Language	P.20	Go Shopping	P.35	Cooking	P.50
My Book	P.56	Independence	P.21	Bath time	P.36	Yoga	P.51
Multi-Sensory	P.57	Attachment	P.22	Eating	P.37	Libraries	P.52
Autism	P.58	Step Children	P.23	Sleep	P.38	Siblings	P.53
A.D.H.D	P.59	Be Connected	P.24	Choices / Consequences	P.39	Jigsaws	P.54
THE FUTURE		De-Escalation	P.25	House Focus	P.40		
i2eye.parentcoaching	P.60	Relax / Arousal	P.26	Music	P.41		
		Zone Of Tolerance	P.27	Attune / Repair	P.42		

HOW IT WORKS 2

This book is divided into 5 sections. Each section interlinks with the next section, with your happy, content, supportive and encouraging family environment being in the very centre. I have not included age related sections because I feel that many of the ideas and strategies can be applied to toddlers, younger children and teenagers. Pick out particular pages within those sections that you are interested in or read the whole section for a better holistic understanding of that section.

Section 1, is the 5 golden pillars of parenting. If you want to improve your parenting then these 5 key pillars are a must. They are based on a 70-year study of 70,000 children by Stanford University, which found that, although society has changed radically over the last 70 years, parenting has not. It found that the level of poverty that the child was born into had a considerably negative effect on what happened to that child in later life, but that good parenting would then have a dramatically positive effect on the child and their future.

Section 2, Connection is key to developing better parenting skills with your children. How do you relate to your children? Do you have quality time with your children? Is your quality time really quality time? You will be surprised how easy it is to strengthen the bond you have with your child as well as creating new ones. Practical experiences based on parenting mistakes made by yours truly.

Section 3, Routine. The more your life and family environment revolves around routines the quicker your child will feel safer, happier, less anxious and better behaved. The foundations of schools are based on routines. The success of schools is their use and respect of routines. You do not have to use routines all the time but at certain times of the day, they can be incredibly useful.

Section 4, Play is a major factor in your child becoming a healthy and well rounded adult in later life. Play is the best way for children to learn about themselves and others. It is a perfect vehicle for filling your children's lives with fun and happiness. A variety of common sense and mostly cheap ideas for adding more play into your children's lives.

Section 5, Special Needs. Many of the ideas and practices used in this section are useful and will be successful with mainstream children of all ages.

SCHOOL (THE FIVE GOLDEN PILLARS)

School is an important part of a child's life. However not the most important part that is YOU, and then your family but school is not that far behind. Your child has all their friends there and will probably get a girlfriend or a boyfriend there. Most of their lives will take place at school. Their victories and their failures, their ups and downs.

No matter what experiences you have had, and there are plenty of people who did not have the best of times at school, your child is not you, the school isn't the school you went to; the teachers who teach your child are not the teachers who taught you. Your child is a wonderfully clean page, a fresh start, a new beginning.

A friend of mine, announced just after his first son was born that his son would have dyslexia. I am not sure how he could tell, but being the coolest, well I think I am, the coolest Grandad in the world, his son and when his younger son came along, they received 3 or 4 books every Christmas. They are 9 and 7 and both love school and both love books. They play wrestling games and Fortnite but they love school.

It is never too early or late whatever your family situation to help your child develop a more positive attitude to learning. When you have children your lives are crazy, super busy but there are simple ways to be more interested in their school day.

Taking up an interest in their school day, and their school work is important. I am not saying, oh, spend hours talking to them, and helping them, I am saying ask them when they get in the car or when they get off the bus - what kind of day have you had? What lessons have you had today. Maybe you use your quality time to read with them, or they read to you, or help with their spellings or letter sounds. Car journeys are great for this because, for your child, there is almost nothing else to do. Just 5 minutes a day will help bring you and your child together and improve their reading or phonic skills.

Being encouraging and supportive is important. Even if you are not as interested as you should be, staying positive is going to help. Children will have good days that you can celebrate and bad days that you can commiserate.

When speaking to your children try and focus on how hard they have worked rather than how clever they are.

QUALITY TIME (THE FIVE GOLDEN PILLARS)

This is probably the most important thing to do with your child or children. If you are doing it, well done, if you are not, then give it a go. Better to spend 10 minutes a day giving them some attention than 60 minutes trying to sort out some kind of strop or bad behaviour, because they have not had any of your attention today.

It is really hard. You are going to be busy and almost everyone is busy keeping it together, making ends meet, juggling all those balls. I did not say it would be easy, it is not but that 10 minutes a day, every day, will make a big difference to you and your child's relationship. If it is an ok day, it will make it a good one, if it is a good one it will make it a great day.

You have to have uninterrupted and regular time together. Quality time together, where you can talk to each other and get to know each other and where your child can see that you are interested in them and their interests and their dreams and their life. Do you know who your child's best friend is or what they did today? When was the last time you did talk to them?

Agree a time in the day to spend 10 minutes with them. The morning is probably too busy, maybe when they get back from school or at the end of the day is better. Ask your child what they think would be a good time. If it is part of your bedtime routine that's a fantastic time to have some quality time.

Ideally, make sure you are in a quiet room, with no distractions, no TV, no mobile devices, no other siblings if that is possible.

Maybe share a book, play a board game or card game. Maybe play a game on the iPad even that works as long as you are doing whatever you're doing together. Even watching a film together, or Netflix will work, it is not perfect but it is better than nothing at all.

In the car is a great time for quality time. Yes, you are driving but why not turn the radio off, take the handheld device out of their hand and start talking.

How are you? How are you feeling? Why are you feeling like that? How was school? Who's your best friend? What subjects do you like? Who is your favourite teacher? Even getting them to just answer your questions is quality time.

READING (THE FIVE GOLDEN PILLARS)

Every child loves reading.

Yes, I have said it out loud now. No matter what, even in today's society, with iPad, iPhone, Switches, Fortnite, this and that and everything, even then children love books.

Books are magical. Books are full of knowledge and wonder and imagination. They are completely submersive, in ways that T.V or video games cannot be. When you are reading, you are not looking around, you are not distracted.

Books improve intelligence dramatically. They are full of facts, but they will develop imagination, help structural thinking and enhance writing and understanding.

Every child loves books. Every child loves reading.

It might be pirate books, cooking and football books or music books. I can go and go because there are literally books for everyone. My oldest is not a great reader but he reads the newspaper and, in particular, the sports pages and unfortunately anything to do with Chelsea, bless him.

The first thing is to have books in the house. Books can be expensive, but second hand books from the charity shops are £1 maybe 50p.

Put books in their room, put books in the living room. We used to have books in the toilet; 'yes' sitting there on the toilet with a book.

Share the book with them, sit next to them. Talk about the book, about the pictures. Your children do not have to read to you, you can read to them. Just 10 minutes at the end of the day, quality time with them. Talk about what they think will happen next? Who is their favourite character? Do they like the story and why?

When you go shopping, go into the bookshop or the second hand shop and ask your child or children to pick a book or even two. Book shops are a great place to let your children go off on their own. You position yourself near the entrance and give them 5 or 10 minutes to have a look. Your children will love that.

Oh, did I mention, children love books.

TRIPS (THE FIVE GOLDEN PILLARS)

Trips out are very important. A variation on spending quality time with your children.

They can take any form from going swimming to going to the library to just looking around the shops.

It does not have to be expensive. Vitamin 'D' is really good for you.

The library is free. Free to go to. Free to join. Free to take books out. As long as you live near to a library, including a regular trip there, is a worthwhile trip out. You can go and sit down whilst your children look around: there is a certain amount of freedom for them at the library.

At one point, I would take my children out for the morning and we would look around the shops, lots of window shopping. We would go to every charity shop, looking at books and I would offer them a pound, back then, for them to spend on one thing, just one thing that they liked and when we looked around all the charity shops and they had decided we would go back to the shop where they remembered their favourite toy would be.

If you have a swimming pool nearby, then that is a wonderful place to visit, as a one off or as part of a routine. I would take the children for a swim on a Sunday evening mostly because Sunday evenings are a bit slow for most people. Swimming on Sunday evening was something to look forward.

Special days out are great. Type into google activities for children or what to do this weekend and there are always plenty of activities to keep everyone entertained.

The beach, if you are lucky enough to live near one, is a super cheap day out. If you take a picnic then the only money you will have to spend is maybe on an ice cream. Maybe buy one activity per trip out, so this time a ball? Then the following time a set of boules and before you know it you have a large selection of activities to use.

The list goes on. Plan your day out but also ask your children to plan your day out, even get them looking on google. Give them a price range and enjoy all this wonderful time together.

FUTURE AMBITIONS (THE FIVE GOLDEN PILLARS)

You are the most important person in the world to your child. No matter what kind of parent you are, good, great or o.k. They will love you forever.

You are a role model to them. If you open the door for them, and you are polite to them at some point they will open the door for you and be polite too. Without you mentioning it or reminding them, they will copy your actions and think sometimes just like you.

What do you want them to do in the future?

What do you think they can do in the future?

Will it be relevant to what you do now?

What do they want to do with their future?

I hope you want better for your child or children. Part of your parenting job is to encourage and make them believe. Being a teacher, I have to believe that nurture, (cared for while growing up) is more powerful than nature, (how you are born).

Have you spoken to them about what they want to do? Even at a young age you can talk about jobs and the future, it is only talk and maybe if they say they are going to be a premiership footballer they may not make it, but they need to be thinking about it and see that you are interested in them and their future.

My Dad came from a working-class family. His Dad was a miner so he could not understand why his son would want to go to university. Initially, he was not as supportive, but he did not stop me going off to be a teacher. I very much appreciated that and he was supportive in his own way, giving me a chance to try it out and not stopping me. He actually paid for me to go and sacrificed the money he would have had for my happiness. By the time my brother and sister were accepted at university, he was much more understanding of it all. That is what it is about, being supportive and giving your child the chance to better themselves, not to reach too far into the sky, but not to stop them and criticise and tease them.

My first 2 children did not want to go to university, I was disappointed but always supportive. They are both very happy.

EXPECTATIONS (CONNECTION)

If you had two students in a class who were of about the same intelligence and the teacher was positive, encouraging and supportive of the one student and negative, dismissive and unsupportive of the other, you would find over time that the student who was being supported and encouraged would be more successful than the student who was being treated in a negative way. That positive child would actually become cleverer over the course of the year and the negative child would become actually less clever.

If you expect your child to be good, they are more likely to be good, if you expect them to be bad then there is a very good chance, they will be bad.

Non-verbal communication, how you stand, how you hold yourself, what you do with your hands, the expression on your face, are all indicators of what you are feeling. It very much is not what you are saying, it is what you are doing with your body. Like the poker players who can read 'tells', in an opponent.

Children are super good at picking up these cues. From when they were a baby, they have sussed you out. The mood you are in, how you are feeling, they may not be able to tell you, but they know. You are almost telling them subconsciously how to behave, without even saying anything. They are picking up clues from you and if they think that you're expecting them to be bad, THEN THEY WILL BE BAD.

Have high expectations of your children. Always try and think the best of them. Of course, that's almost impossible with the kind of day we quite often have, but understand as much as you can.

Remember the way your child is acting might have something to do with the way you are behaving or the expectations you have of your child in a certain situation.

Children will always surprise you in good ways and in bad ways. But if you are expecting them to behave in a certain way, they are more likely to be like that.

The next time your child is 'playing up', try and step back and think about whether you're expecting them to be 'playing up'.

You might be surprised by what you find.
BEHAVIOUR (CONNECTION)

Working in a special needs school, many students are non-verbal and don't talk. There are other ways to communicate, which students and schools use. Surprisingly behaviour is a form of communication.

Your child will be able to talk more than likely, but if they are young or teenagers, or if they are too angry or too upset then you have to look at their behaviour and try and work out why they are behaving as they are and what they are trying to tell you.

A simple example is my dog often barks. He is barking for a reason. He wants to go outside; he wants to sit on the sofa or the cats are there. He will keep on barking until I work out what is wrong with him.

Begin with what happened just before the behaviour started. My son would get home from school and be really irritable and moody and rude. I realised that the school had lunch a little earlier and that he would then be hungry over the course of the afternoon. Everyone gets irritable and moody if they are not eating regularly. I started to make sandwiches or a snack that was waiting for him. I would try not to be confrontational straight after he got home, because if I am moaning at him and he is irritable then he is going to get more irritable. I would leave whatever I had to say until about 30 mins after he got home, giving the food a chance to take effect.

Maybe, like above, if the behaviour happens at the same time every day there could be something that at that point in the day can be changed.

Consider the type of behaviour that is occurring. What does the behaviour look like? Is it lower level behaviour, or much higher, more aggressive behaviour? Can the behaviour be changed? Not stopped but can be changed. Your child needs a coping strategy for that behaviour.

And finally, what is the consequence of the behaviour? Do you give in? Does your child get extra attention? My older grandson will be mean to his brother sometimes if I am doing something with his brother. I have to then stop and either tell him off or deal with his behaviour, so giving him attention which is what he wanted. Better to explain I am going to spend time with one grandson for 20 minutes and then play with the other grandson. He knows he is going to get his attention so he will not be mean.

MAKING MISTAKES (CONNECTION)

Number One, you are going to get this wrong. I am writing this down right now, THAT'S OK. You can get it wrong. You are going to get it wrong, everyone, but everyone does. Yes, me too, all the time, every other day.

'Getting it wrong' is going to make you a better person, a better parent. It is really good that your children 'SEE' that you're getting it wrong. They need to know that you're not some perfect being. They will admire you and love you anyway, but to respect you they need to know you are going to have a bad day sometimes.

You can tell them or possibly warn them that your feeling off today or feeling down in someway or something else has happened to put you in a bad mood. They need to know it is not them, that has put you in a bad mood. You don't need to go through how your feeling constantly.

I had a friend whose ex-partner would have the children every other weekend. The boys were 7 and 9. One weekend his partner split up with him. He then spent the weekend crying and being upset which is understandable but he did it while his very young and very emotionally weak children were with him. They were weak, not in the sense of themselves but trying to deal with their Dad being upset and distraught. This powerful and incredibly important person should not be needing his very young children to support him.

The secret is to learn from that, 'getting it wrong'. It really is, if you take nothing else from this book. Learn from your mistakes.

Your children will make mistakes, and they will learn from those mistakes. You will have to help them learn because especially young children, do not know what the right way is. That's part of your job.

If your children are making mistakes, is it all their fault? I am sorry but quite often it will be your fault. I know that does not make complete sense but it is true. Sometimes you will ask too much of them, not explain as clearly as you can, your expectations will be all wrong.

I do not want you going over the top and analysing every single thing you say and do. Keep to the big things or, maybe, when you have some time to then stop and reflect.

CONSISTENCY (CONNECTION)

This is probably the hardest element of the whole book to manage. Consistency is part of this important structure that your child needs to grow up in. They need to know that if they do a small thing wrong then the punishment is a small punishment every time and if they do a big thing wrong then there needs to be a bigger punishment, not a small punishment and not a reward. They need to trust you and your judgement. Your children will learn that consistency too. Even as adults we hate inconsistency. Your boss at work has a really bad go at you about a spelling mistake. You are not going to want to work there.

Consistency is not just about you and your partner, but also how you manage each day and every day, each dispute and every dispute.

As I have mentioned earlier in the book, you will make mistakes.

Consistency with your partner is all to do with talking to each. Talking, talking and more talking. If your partnership is male / female then this is harder, because I believe that men and women have very different outlooks to each other. This is actually an advantage in many situations and there is lots of research to suggest that the combination can work really well.

15

My wife and I argued constantly about bringing up the children, which is a good sign. I would prefer a more open ended and independent ethos, where she would suggest a more supportive and nurturing ethos. Who's right, here, yes you have guessed, it is somewhere in between. Some situations require more nurturing and support for your children and some require more independence and risk based.

Your own personal consistency will be tested every day. The car has gone wrong, the dog has just been sick and you are trying to make a dentist appointment. Anyone will react differently to a day where the sun is shining, you have just won £100 on the lottery. But you have to find a way to be consistent.

Small punishments are for small mistakes.

Big punishments are for big mistakes.

I always kept a little score sheet in my head. Was that a small thing, or a middle thing or a big thing and then you decide how to deal with it.

YOU'RE IN CHARGE (CONNECTION)

This might sound a little obvious, but it is not. YOU ARE IN CHARGE.

Every child thinks they want to be in charge but really, they do not.

You have a responsibility to bring up those children as best you can. It is not your friend's responsibility, or the school's, or the doctor's, it is actually yours. Your children are yours and although this will be the hardest thing you ever do, if you're doing it well, and I know you will, it will be the very best thing you do. You have created a life, a baby, but you then have to bring up that child in a way that they enjoy their life and have a good life. It is not enough to just make a baby, you then have to make a person.

You are in charge of the environment that your children will grow up in. That environment is there to teach your child, to guide your child, to help grow your child into their own person. The environment has to be mostly geared to your children and their needs. If you don't like this then why have children. I use the word mostly because you and your partner need to fit into this environment too. There needs to be a balance between your own needs and your childrens'. The better behaved your children are the easier it is. Your lives can all fit together in this wonderful jigsaw, but you are the driving force, which works or fails on you.

16

Be fair, be supportive and listen to what your children say, but you are in charge. You make the decisions but involve or include your children as much as you feel you can. They should not be making all the decisions, they cannot, they are children and even teenagers should not be, and although they might moan about it, they will love and respect you more if you are making the decisions.

Try not to change your mind. Your children need to know that once your mind is made up, it is made up. Changing your mind makes you look weak and the last thing you want is to look weak in front of them. The more you change your mind, the more likely they will think they can change your mind and the more they will play up.

You can be friendly with your children, but you cannot be their friend. I am really sorry; it just does not work like that. I suppose it is like being friends with your boss at work. Is that going to work? NO.

When they grow up to be great adults you can you be their friend.

ROLE MODEL (CONNECTION)

Children are sponges, they soak up absolutely everything around them, good or bad.

You are your child's best role model. They love their teachers and will pretend to be them or their favourite sports person or their favourite singer or Fortnite star but you, Mum or Dad, that is who they will learn from and who they will aspire too.

Being a role model is a full-time job. Your children will be watching and learning all the good stuff you do and all the bad stuff you do, you do not have to tell a child how to behave. Your children are tuned into you and will pick up all kinds of behaviour from you, from swearing to standing in a certain way and to dealing with each other in a certain way.

How are you with other people? How are you with your own children?

Short and sharp with them, aggressive and rude, swearing and shouting, your children could well pick that up. How do your children behave? How do you behave?

I once told a year 10 student off when working at a special needs school. I kept to my above remit of small 'telling off' when it was small and big 'telling off' when it was a big thing. The boy had touched a girl's legs under the table, so that is really bad. I started to tell him if off, but he was not reacting how I wanted him to so I started shouting at him. He then started shouting back, and kept shouting; why - because I was shouting at him. He thought because I was the teacher that if I was shouting then he should follow my lead and start shouting too. I stopped shouting after that.

Try and be calm and patient. Try and be happy and positive. Try and fix your behaviour. You are the adult here. Is there anything apart from actually hurting someone or themselves that would warrant you going crazy mad.

I know you cannot be like this every day, that is impossible, but managing your behaviour is going to help every situation, and if you are reacting in a loud or angry way your children will take those behaviour signposts.

Try and be a little more reflective about your own behaviour.

ARE YOU LISTENING? (CONNECTION)

Listening is an important skill in knowing your children, knowing how they feel, knowing what they are doing. Your children are always changing, always, I know they're the same but their lives are dynamic, things will change for them, new friends, they might be having a good day or a bad day.

Children love your attention. If you are talking to them, you are giving them some quality attention.

Listening gives you a lot of credibility. Children want to know you are there for them. They want to know you care about them.

Listening keeps you updated in terms of how they are doing, how they feel, why they feel like that. As a parent you don't want any surprises. You do not want to find out suddenly that your children are being bullied.

Do not ask leading questions. Questions that lead your child. "Are you being bullied at school?", your child will think that they have to give you an answer related to bullying. They will think that you are expecting some answers related to bullying. It is better to ask "How are you feeling?"

Do not take seriously everything your child says. Children do make things up and they do stretch truths, not because they are bad or naughty but because that's what children do. They might be in a bad mood or they may have fallen out with a particular child and want them to get into

18

trouble. 30 years of teaching and 20 years of bringing up children tells me that.

The best way to do that is to ask them how they are? How is school? What are they doing at school? Who their friends are? What is their favourite lesson? Then listening to what they say, then ask another question and listen.

A constant drip, drip is the best way. Maybe talking in the car on the way home, maybe finding 5 minutes while they eat their dinner. It is better to be proactive in this situation than not bothering when suddenly, they're looking for your attention in other ways.

Children are actually really funny; you will find yourself writing down what they say or telling your friends.

POSITIVE LANGUAGE (CONNECTION)

Another aspect of the environment you are setting up within the family is how you speak to your children. Negative speaking, sets negative expectations, whereas, positive speaking sets up positive expectations. Sometimes you have to be negative, you have to be upset and you might have to 'tell' your children off. I am not saying do not be nicey-nicey all the time; your children do have to see that sometimes you're upset, they have to see that sometimes you are not happy. Rephrasing how you speak will potentially help you.

Being positive and speaking positively is supportive to an encouraging, nurturing and happy environment. Your children want to feel safe at home with you. They will be aware that when the doors are shut or locked, they are physically safe. But they will want to feel emotionally safe too. The terminology you use will have an impact on them.

Swearing is a very easy case of negative language. I am not opposed to swearing, I swear and swear in front of my children. I tried really hard not to do that when they were young. The problem is that if you start swearing and using those words in your day to day lives, then at some point very soon your children will do the same thing. You are a role model, so anything you say to them at some point they will use against you or use in front of you. Always saying 'NO' to a child, will only ever put yourself in a situation or a number of situations where, you say "Oh, can you help me with the washing up?", guess what they will then say, "NO".

When telling off your children try and emphasise the negative behaviour, instead of your actual child. "I love you, but I don't like how you are treating your toy"is better than "What are you playing at, that toy cost me £40 and you are jumping up and down on it." Can you see the difference there, firstly it is a softer approach and a less confrontational way of dealing with lower level negative behaviour? Secondly, it focuses on the behaviour rather than the child. Thirdly, it is reminding the child of the value of the toy to themselves.

Many autistic children will only hear the last word you say. So, if you say "Stop shouting", they will only hear "shouting", whereas if you say "Can you speak quietly," they will only hear the word, "quietly". Your child probably does not have autism, but sometimes mainstream children will only hear the last word in the same way, when asking for directions, you might only hear the last part of the instructions.

INDEPENDENCE (CONNECTION)

My main goal, overall, for all my children was for them to be independent. This might not be your main goal, that is ok. Maybe think of one goal for them, to be sociable, to be happy, to be healthy or something else. You actually find that schools and classrooms are geared up for your children to be more independent.

I wanted my children to be able to be independent, to be self-reliant and to be able to get on without me. This obviously took the whole of their lives up to 18. I did not throw them in at the deep end, for example when they were 3, "ok, you are going to do this and you're going to do that". No, that is not how it happened.

I started by not playing with them all the time. I do not think parents should be playing with their children constantly. Children have to learn to get on with themselves and, although it is a joy to be playing with them, they have to learn to play on their own. Sorry, I hope I do not sound mean, I love children and loved my children when they were babies, but they are going to be on their own for quite a lot of their lives. I think they have to learn that you are not going to be there for them forever, because you are not.

I would try and leave them to their own company as much as often, I would just leave them to it. Of course, if they were screaming, then yes, I would go to them, but I would not have them in my arms all the time and I would not be interacting with them all the time.

I tried to involve them in tidying up, when I was tidying up and then cooking, when I was cooking.

I would take them shopping and ask them to go and get certain foods for me, maybe rewards would be used, maybe not.

As they grew up, I added smaller chores that they would take responsibility for.

And finally, I constantly talked about when they were older. I wouldn't say "right you lot you're out of here at 18" or "your Mum and I can't wait to get rid of you". I don't think those statements are very nice, but I would say "I'm so excited, when you leave about 18, me and your Mum are going to sell the house, get a camper van and drive round the world, Wow we can't wait." That suggests that they will have to get on with it, more than they just having to go.

ATTACHMENT (CONNECTION)

Attachment is a key aspect of parenting and one that, for the most part, happens naturally. It is a deep and enduring bond that occurs no matter where you are in the world or how many years you are alive. This attachment in early life with your parents can have a long-lasting effect on you, through your own life. Attachment behaviour in adults towards the child includes responding sensitively and appropriately to the child's needs. Such behaviour appears universally across cultures.

There are 4 types of attachment styles which will help you decide which you are and help you have better relationships in the future.

Avoidance. This is a child or adult who feels deep discomfort when having to be around people. It may involve avoiding eye contact in certain intimate situations or avoiding hugs and physical contact. This might be one parent or both being physically around, but not being emotionally available. Putting yourself in more situations where telling someone in person how you feel will help.

Anxious. These children or adults feel the loss of connection. They will be in a relationship or will hop from one relationship to another. These people can become obsessional. They will cling tightly to their partner. Finding a hobby that is unconnected to a partner is a good strategy for overcoming these feelings.

Fearful. Very few children or adults have this. It manifests itself as unpredictability and self-sabotage. They can bounce between anxious behaviour, with people pleasing and avoidance behaviour. Children and adults cannot believe that anyone would want to be with them. Childhood trauma may be the cause of this. Professional guidance will help.

21

Secure. These children and adults have the fortitude to deal with loss. These relationships are driven by fear. Secure types can trust others to see them in vulnerable situations. If they disagree, they will do so in a calm manner. When they work with others, they do not have one size fits all solution.

These are not set in stone and you can change. At no point is this section about pointing fingers and commenting on your parenting skills. Remember you are a great parent and this knowledge will help you become a better one.

STEP CHILDREN (CONNECTION)

I met my step children at the age of 28. They were 8 and 5 respectively. I had no experience of having my own children. The only experience of children was being a teacher. I made a lot of mistakes over the next 20 years, and still make the occasional one now. Ellie and Josh both have their own children now. Ellie in particular seems to have picked many of the ideas and strategies I used with them. They are both great parents, Josh has his own step daughter and step son.

The greatest compliment I have received is that my daughter included my name in her youngest son's name and the speech my son made at his wedding about all of his parents, and the fact that I sat next to his biological Dad, brings tears to my eyes even now.

I say all of this because, even though it was as tough as tough could be, we all got through it together. We are one family together and, yes, they have another family, but that is ok with me. In fact, they have their own families too.

You are not going to replace their Dad or Mum. You are not even if they are not around right now, they will appear at some point.

You are actually going to fit into what is going on already. You are not going to throw your weight around. You are going to watch and understand how your partner manages their children. You are going to support them and talk to your partner whenever anything needs to be sorted out.

The 'STEP' is a horrible word. I did not enjoy being referred to by this term. Yes, some people use it ok, but I always felt it had very negative connotations. Grimm's fairy tales spring to mind. You are going to create the idea that you are a family together. Most of my friends think I have 4 children, I introduce my children, as my children.

What are they going to call you? I was Papa. Try and get on with your partners ex-partner.

Get to know your children. That is your main job, get to know them, get to understand them. Find activities that you can do together. Build a relationship, slowly and as carefully as you can.

Remember their behaviour will be about being a teenager or a child rather than it being personal to you.

BE CONNECTED (CONNECTION)

This starts from the moment your child is born.

Talking to your child, interacting with your child as much as you can. Children want that interaction; children need that interaction.

Children love you to copy them. You do something; then they do the same thing back. Toddlers and young children will enjoy you repeating what they say too.

Catching their attention, smiling and talking to them, jigging them around, stroking their head, or the ridge of their nose is important. You playing with their toys, playing with them playing with their toys. Children need to see how to play and to interact. It is a learnt skill. But it does not have to be so stimulating all the time.

I used to put my daughter on my chest and lie on the sofa either reading a book or watching a film. The fact I was next to her, that I was connected to her, I always felt was enough.

Being emotionally warm. Smiling is a wonderful way to engage with your children in a positive way. You smile at them; they will smile back at you.

Saying "hello', "good morning", are again, positive ways to start conversations or interactions, and yes it should be you that sets the tone of the day, even if you're not feeling it. You lead in every way and your children will follow. Be negative and they will be more likely to be negative.

Be comforting and reassuring. Speak, when possible, slowly and calmly.

Try and look at your children as you speak to them. Do not talk to them behind a laptop screen or with your head looking down at a phone. Stop what you are doing and concentrate on them. If you are in the car with your children, turn the radio down.

Be an active listener. Remember to look at your children and nod your head as they speak. To be honest, sometimes I was too tired, or very distracted by something else. I would then say "really", when they finished talking or "I didn't know that". That way, it would seem like really, I would not be.

DE-ESCALATION (CONNECTION)

This is related to anger and upset. This can be related to you or your child. There is going to be anger and upset. No matter how much your family loves each other, being in an enclosed space, your house on rainy or boring days can create difficult situations.

Getting upset and angry is ok. Everyone gets upset and angry at some point. We are all human and bad days can get worse and good days can change just like that.

It is not the getting angry, although you must consider why that is and whether it will happen again, but more importantly it is how you and your children deal with it. It is the choices you make afterwards that will decide if that day gets worse or better.

Children who have become angry or upset will need time to calm down. They will need about 45 minutes to calm down. At any point in those 45 minutes the children are very susceptible and sensitive to further angry outbursts. You do really have to leave them alone and let them cool off, before going through what has happened.

Do not do these things: Have the last word, stare your children out, focus on the 'you' statements, like "You need to stop right now," get visibility angry, raise your voice, go on and on about the problem in front of your children, dig in your heels, be critical of every minor mistake, be sarcastic and dominate the conversation. All these actions will make the situation far worse.

Instead, try and distract your children. This is not completely ignoring them but is giving them the chance to calm down. Start talking about a new film that is coming out, or have you seen my watch? Just something to take their minds off what has just happened.

Try and work out what trigger has set them off. Consider if the trigger can be got rid of, or changed or softened.

Make your child feel safe. Try and talk calmly and quietly. Have a calm manner about you. Try and make the space your child is in as quiet and calm as possible.

Never act without explaining what you are doing. Talk through what you are going to do and why you are doing it.

RELAXATION / AROUSAL CYCLE (CONNECTION)

The parent child relationship is the most important relationship in our lives.

Children who are securely attached tend to be more socially constructive and less aggressive in their behaviour, are more empathetic, show greater creativity and persistence in meeting life's challenges, learn more easily, and are generally better able to cope with difficulties than are children who are insecurely attached.

The infant attachment cycle includes the baby has a need, the baby cries, parent then gives the baby what they want, the baby then trusts parent, then it begins again with the baby having another need and so on. This cycle can be described in another way. Arousal, the baby has a need, more arousal and the baby cries until they get that need met. The need is met, the baby relaxes, the baby trusts the adult or parent and is more relaxed.

This process is training your child's nervous system to react in a certain way. It is training it to be aroused, then more aroused than relaxed, then more relaxed.

The second process going on is called Stimulating, where the parent or adult engages with the baby. Children need external input that is rich in sensory detail and pleasure.

As your baby grows, it will begin to self-regulate itself using the training that the parent has exposed it to.

If the infant cycle is distorted or broken, the baby has a need, baby cries and the parent does not satisfy that need or becomes angry or inconsistent, there will be mistrust and a weaker attachment will be created. The child will become aroused, when they have a need, they will become even more aroused, when they cry as normal, but then will continue to be aroused, because their needs have not been met, and they do not trust their parents.

This then affects the child's nervous system and how they grow up to regulate their own nervous system. They will be trained to move through the relaxation part of the cycle much quicker because they are not expecting that. Children will stay in the arousal part of the cycle for longer and will be more anxious and possibly angry much quicker and for longer.

ZONE OF TOLERANCE (CONNECTION)

Also known as the window of tolerance.

Your child's brain is made up of 3 parts.

The brain-stem is developed in the womb and is the part of the brain that deals with danger. This is where your 'fight', 'flight' or 'freeze' response comes from. The second part of the brain to develop is at 9 months and is called the Limbic brain. This part of the brain deals with your child's emotional maturity, their behaviour control and so affects their relationship. The third part of the brain is developed by the age of 25 and is called the Cortical brain. This part of the brain deals with language, learning, information processing, planning and morality.

Each child has a unique window of tolerance. These windows will be different sizes and shapes. While the child is in their window of tolerance, they will feel safe and happy, they can think, express themselves, be playful, reflect and be empathetic.

When they feel pushed out of their window of tolerance, either by being pushed to the top of their window, (hyper-arousal), or the bottom of their window, (hypo-aroused), their Cortical brain gets disconnected from the rest of their brain. Without that part of the brain working they then swing from the brain-stem to the limbic brain, causing them distress. They can be pushed out of their window a little, mild stress or a lot, severe stress.

Every child has a unique trigger for them leaving their window of tolerance.

When in the Hyper-arousal phase, their brain feels that they will have to 'fight', 'flight' or 'freeze'. On the inside they feel ill, have body pains, feel anxious, angry or overwhelmed. On the outside they seem angry, controlling, obsessive or anxious. When in the hypo-aroused phase, they will feel empty, dead, disconnected and flat. On the outside they will appear withdrawn, moody, emotionless and unable to engage.

Our childs' window of tolerance may be bigger or smaller, but as parents our jobs are to try and expand our child's window of tolerance.

We can do this by helping them learn to notice their feelings, communicate their feelings and support them to manage their feelings.

MY TIME (ROUTINE)

My time or parent time is very important. You need down time, you need a break, you need a rest from your children.

As we have said being a parent is really hard work. Being a great parent, because that is what you are, is even harder. Children are relentless. Whatever age they are, from being a toddler to being a teenager, children want your attention, they need your attention and one way or another they will get your attention. They very much want a chunk of you for good or for bad. The relationship is always going to be intense. They are bundles of hormones and anxieties, and that will be tiring and exhausting and, without a break, almost impossible to deal with.

Some parents would disagree, but of course you need a break and, even if you do not feel like you deserve one. There will be no harm in having a break and especially if it means you can go back to your children fresh, rested and relaxed.

What's better for the child, time on their own or you getting upset and maybe shouting at them?

My time would start at 7.30pm. That would be the time that the children, all the children would go to bed; not go to sleep but would go to bed. I would say "good night" and they would go up to bed.

I would make sure I was not doing anything exciting or loud. Who wants to go to bed when their parents are having a party or watching a film? There has to be a time limit, 30 minutes, 45 minutes and then I would go and make sure everything was off, tuck the children in, wish them goodnight and turn the lights out in their room. Maybe have a light on just outside.

This will take some training if your children do not do this now. It will not happen overnight and is something you will have to work on for at least 6 months and, even then, there are going to be nights when it doesn't work very well. KEEP GOING WITH IT. It is actually very important. They will begin by checking up on you, and trying to break this new set of rules. You can even reward them, maybe have a 'stay up later night' on a Friday. They need activities that will keep them amused but not be too stimulating. Reading is GREAT or looking at books. Colouring in, cards, playing with their toys or listening to music.

BOUNDARIES (ROUTINE)

As you reconsider and fine tune your parenting environment the boundaries you set will be the building blocks of that environment.

I cannot tell you to set your boundaries at this level or at that level because as a great and unique parent, your boundaries are going to based very much on you, maybe your upbringing, what your children are like and very much what you can manage.

Like all targets, they have to be realistic. Do not decide that your children should sit in silence all day and every day, that is going to be very hard to sustain.

Your boundaries have to be explained and understood by your children. It is always useful for them to come up with some of the boundaries.

They have to be agreed by everyone. The boundaries have to be reinforced and your children reminded, not every day, not every other day but every so often. You have to talk it through with them, when and where it is needed. "Remember what we agreed about how late you can stay up, we are getting close to that time. You need to get ready to go to bed now."

You and your partner need to be willing to consistently manage them. You are a team and teams work together. Never undermine the other parent especially in front of your children. Always agree in public and disagree in private.

Try to never change the boundary completely. Sometimes you will have to be flexible, that is ok, as long as you tell your children that this is what is happening and that you do not then turn it into a constant thing. "Ok, today I am going to let you do that, but I'm not going to do this again".

Remember that your children will always push against any boundary you put in place, but this is because they are children, rather than not needing or respecting that boundary. Children feel secure knowing that you will keep the boundary and the moment you start to change those boundaries then is the time that your children will begin not to trust you and respect you. They will begin to feel insecure and possibly anxious.

PLAN YOUR DAY (ROUTINE)

Part of this safe and secure environment you have set up is knowing what comes next.

This is a powerful part of school life, every child knowing exactly what is going to happen over the course of that day and then the whole week and this affects every teacher in every classroom across the world.

Children feel reassured and safe. Even though I will have gone through the day with them, they will still want to be reminded. I will see them looking at the board, the plan for the day will be on the board, quite often as little pictures and I will see them looking and talking to themselves about what's next.

So, if you wanted to explain to your children what they are doing after school today or what is going to happen on Saturday, that would always be useful and actually beneficial to their well-being. You would explain at the beginning of the day and then every so often just remind them. "Oh, don't forget we are going shopping after school" or "we have the dentist on Saturday morning".

Even if you are not sure what you are doing that afternoon or morning, explain to your children that you are not sure what is going on. As a teacher I used to have an "oops time", that is "oops" I don't know what's happening next or I haven't planned anything. Even though the students did not know what would be happening at that point in the day, I had still planned for the fact I did not know what was going to happen.

You being organised will also help them be more organised too.

Children find transitioning, moving from one place to another or from one activity to another really hard. PLEASE, PLEASE warn them when you are changing activity or place. "In five minutes, we are going out" or "You can play for another 2 minutes and then you have to tidy up".

Buy a cork board, or get an A3 sheet of paper laminated and each day write down what you are doing. It does not have to be detailed as that is too much information for them.

Your children will love it. You can involve them in this process to, "what shall we do on Saturday morning, shall we do this or that?"

IN THE MORNINGS (ROUTINE)

The morning is the start of the day and in reality, the start of your routine-based day. As I keep saying routines will make your life so so easy. You and your children will, over the course of time, both start to fit comfortably into the routines you set up. Yes, children love trying to break routines, not because they are 'naughty' or 'bad' but more because they like testing the boundaries you put in place. They want to feel safe and secure and will be testing and checking your commitment to them through routines.

The mornings of any family probably anywhere in the world will be hectic, maybe chaotic and always intense.

As with all routines, make sure it will work. Start slowly and build up what you want to happen in a controlled way.

Make sure there is plenty of time to prep your children on what is happening and then give them time to transition from one part of the morning to the next.

You need to be organised. You need to be ready before they are getting ready or almost ready. This will mean you are more relaxed and so will make them more relaxed. You being calmer and happier will make breakfast calmer and happier.

Waking up your children. I would always go into their rooms 15 minutes before their alarm is going to sound and wake them up. "Morning Fox, your alarm is going to go off in about 15 minutes, then you are going to have to get up and get changed before your breakfast" or ask them, "Do you want toast or cereal for breakfast this morning?". I might remind them what we are doing today. Something that engages their brain in a positive morning way. Thus, giving them 15 minutes or so just to get going. I think about how I want to wake up and it is not, with the alarm going off, then getting up and out of bed at that moment.

They do not have to get ready before they have breakfast, if you want to do that the other way that is fine. If they are younger, you will be in the bathroom helping them have a wash or clean their teeth.

I would set the breakfast table with food and drink. You do not have to have breakfast every morning together. Maybe do that at the weekend when again you have time to enjoy that. There is nothing positive about everyone being rushed and stressed.

BEDTIME (ROUTINE)

Children need sleep. Children need a lot of sleep. I see it at school every day, children sitting there yawning, distracted and not focused.

All these children need is a good routine at bedtime, a routine that you keep to every day. You can have a slightly different routine for the weekends but those routines then have to be kept too.

You should try very hard to adhere to the routine once you have started it. So that might mean cutting short visits from friends or coming home early from a family member. It is really good for your children and it is really good for you.

Bath time should be part of this routine. Soaking in a nice warm bath is very relaxing and helpful to falling asleep.

No phones or social media. The press and much research suggests that blue light and stimulation will keep your children awake at night, even when they do not want to be. I used to turn off the WIFI but 4G/5G is available. Many phones now have a time lock on them. A positive non-confrontational conversation where the 2 of you discuss and debate an appropriate approach is the best way forward.

Do not include food in their bedtime routine as this wakes them up. My children would constantly want something to eat at night time purely because when you are tired you want food to give you energy to not feel tired. A hot drink can be good for sleeping, without sugar.

The bedtime routine when your children are younger is about giving them activities that are quiet and relaxing and not stimulating. To begin with I would come and lie down next to my children to get their bodies into that routine. I would try not to talk to them, talking to your Mum or Dad is stimulating. But Mum or Dad watching a film quietly is not.

Having siblings in the same room is much harder. I would have one child in their room and one child in your room until they have both gone to bed, again they are not stimulating each other or arguing with each other which many tired children do.

For older children, especially teenagers, it is a matter of getting their phones or games turned off.

REWARD CHART (ROUTINE)

Reward charts are not really in vogue at the moment. I have used them and found them brilliant. I have found a bit of this will work better than none of it or too much of it.

Have a focus for the reward chart. Have just one focus, it is there for one thing and one thing only. Do not try to solve the world with one reward chart. Focus on one element of your child's behaviour, be it at bed time, or swearing or tidying their room. NEVER TAKE A STICKER AWAY. It is about accumulating stickers. It is about rewarding good behaviour not punishing bad behaviour.

OK, so the focus is going to bed at bed time. First discuss with your child what the reward chart is, then why you want their behaviour to change. Ask them what they think about this? "Do you think it is important to go to bed at a certain time?". Explain how your child will get stickers. Ask your child what stickers they want? Superman stickers, Mario stickers, one of my students at school wanted Donald Trump, great. Either find them on google and print out or buy a magazine where you will find them.

10 stickers, is always a good number. If they are younger maybe try 5 stickers. Remember you are giving the stickers out for that one and only reason.

Agree on a reward. I would not make it too big a thing. A magazine from the shop, a mini Lego figure. The last thing you want to do is give your child a chance to fail. Too many stickers with this massive reward will only mean they are taking too long to get to it and getting fed up, or finding it too hard to do and then giving up. YOU DO NOT WANT THEM GIVING UP.

In actual fact the first time they go through this process makes it a little easier. So, whatever happens in the days that follow, they can smash up the living room, break all your expensive china, but as long as they go to bed on time, they get that sticker, no matter what.

It may seem old fashioned but it works. It may feel like blackmail, but it works. It is not compromising your parenting skills; it is just helping you out. Your parenting skills and strategies are big and varied and this is just another strategy to try. But do not just let them have a sticker for nothing.

CHORES (ROUTINE)

Chores are another way of developing those beautiful routines, I am always talking about. It is a way to keep them busy, children with too much time on their hands always end up getting into some kind of trouble.

Chores are good for your development in later life. Your children will be able to look after themselves and their children. They will find getting a job much easier and find holding down a job much easier. Again, I am not saying that it is the end of the world if they do not do chores, but it will certainly help.

Start small. Start by encouraging your children to help you, doing washing up or tidying up your room. Try not to make it a big thing and it, try not to push your children too hard. Just a little bit here and a bit there.

Make the chores, small, easy to do and will not take long. Children have very small attention spans, so asking them to paint the fence is not going to happen because they do not want it to happen. They will just find it too hard to do. If you want them to do a big job, break it down into smaller parts; this week can you paint those two posts, please.

While your children are younger it is almost just the idea that they do chores as much as actually doing the chores. They have to feel that they are contributing to the common goal, which is the house and your family, that will boost their self-worth fantastically and reinforce their position within the family.

Organise a little rota, something that is written down. Something that your children can refer to.

In doing chores, your children are working for you. If you feel it is appropriate, then pay them for their work. It should not be a lot and can be pocket money, or it can be extra time on their games console or social media, but it should not be too much and should reflect what they are doing. Again, children having their own money and deciding what they want to buy, or what they want to save for, is great practice for when they grow up.

So, give the chores a chance. See how it goes. Maybe, just have chores at weekends or in holidays. School time is very busy and intense.

GO SHOPPING (ROUTINE)

I always enjoyed taking my children to the shops. I know this might sound slightly deluded but I did.

Supermarkets are great wide spaces for your children to let off some steam. I hope you do not think this sounds bad, but especially on rainy days, I would take them to the supermarket and of course they would have a good run around.

The first thing to do is to give your children a box of grapes. As you walk around the supermarket, they are going to get hungry seeing all that lovely food; much better than giving them chocolate. Doing the shopping will take you about 40 minutes, and it helps to kill the time. The fruit is always in the first section of the supermarket, so strawberries or blueberries will do too. Do not forget to pay for the fruit.

Training your children to help you do the shopping is not as hard as you think. It will only need 4 or 5 trips worth of training and, once you get them sorted, they will help you and make your shopping a more pleasant experience.

The most basic version of shopping with the children is they sit in the trolley or help push the trolley and you do all the work.

Ask your children to go and get certain objects. In the fruit section ask them to get a packet of apples or a bag of bananas.

The next stage is, when they are older, to ask them to get the cheapest toilet paper. The secret to knowing what is cheaper is by the 'per sheet' and looking at per sheet and the weight, supermarkets will change the weight from kilograms (kg) to grams, (gr). This is more of a practiced skill but it will be really good for their life skills in later life, if you can manage to teach them this. I know some adults who do not know this supermarket trick.

If your children come with you, you should reward them, especially if they have been helpful. A magazine, remember what I said earlier about reading, is perfect.

Do not go for sweets or chocolate. These are filling for a while but because your body burns the sugar fast you go from hyper children to then really sleepy children, which you do not want when shopping.

BATHTIME (ROUTINE)

Bathing is great for your health and your children's health. It is wonderful for hydrating your body and hair; cleansing your skin; regulating your core temperature; not only does a warm bath make the blood flow easier, but when you are submerged in water, it can reduce pain and inflammation and also calm the nervous system, reducing the levels of stress and anxiety in the body.

Bath time can be a lovely part of the day. For the most part, it is a great element of your bedtime routine. I feel that this is the best time although your children may want it to be part of the morning routine instead.

Some children will want a shower instead. I feel that showers are almost the opposite of baths. Whereas baths are relaxing and tiring which is great for bedtime, showers are stimulating and energising, probably better for the mornings. So yes, if your children want a shower that is great but make it in the mornings and then a little bath, if possible, in the evenings.

Sometimes your children will need a bath at different times of the day. Please do not ignore those, for the routine. If they have been out in the garden in the evening and are covered in mud and their bath time is not until later, that's ok. Obviously, they will need a bath, there and then. Just explain to your children why they are having the bath now instead of later. If they are dirty at lunchtime then you can probably get away with a bath and then a quick bath later.

If you are introducing bath time to your children, take it slowly and even a quick dip is a start. Being part of the routine, remember children love routines, is the key to developing the bath time. Just the fact that you are making time for a bath, will slowly influence your children to start having baths, and then enjoying that bath.

Young children should not be left alone. Older children should be left alone, especially if they have siblings. I always found having a bath after a long day just gave me some much-needed alone time.

Make it fun. Buying toys or adding saucepans, different types of containers for pouring, children love pouring or whisks or spoons and this will make their bath time more interesting. Do not have the same activities every night, the children will get bored, but have a little routine, so kitchen equipment on a Monday, toys on a Wednesday.

EATING (ROUTINE)

Obesity is on the rise in children at an astronomical rate. Almost 1 in 5 children are overweight or obese when they start primary school, rising to 1 in 3 when they start secondary school. By 2020 it is estimated half of all children will be overweight or obese. Obese children are much more likely to be obese adults, causing significant health risks as well as low self-esteem and body image.

Many children and families today have busy schedules. These make it hard to sit down to homemade meals every day. My wife and I both had jobs, so tried to have a proper meal, a meal that one of us cooked from basically scratch every other day. It was a rule that we agreed we could manage and for the most kept to. Sitting down is another great excuse to be all together. Actually, it is really good because it is very regimented. The food is made, the places are set, everyone sits down, everyone eats, you are at a table, everyone chats and there is a time for adults and children to interact, then everyone finishes and then it is all tidied up. TRY AND SIT down for meals at least 3 to 4 times a week. Again, pick and choose when you are going to do this.

Many childrens' diets involve a lot of convenience and takeaway food, but these foods can be unhealthy. Leave fresh fruit around the house. Just do not buy biscuits or crisps. I love love crisps and could eat them all day. I do not buy them, because if they're in the house, I will eat them. Your children aren't missing out on these foods and you are not a bad parent if you do not have them in the house. Eating healthy also means avoiding foods with high amounts of added salt and sugar.

Introducing new foods or new ways to eat again take time. Do not rush these new and better routines. Start slowly, when you have time, when you can be charming and patient. Do not just drop your children into it, give them time to change their old bad routines into healthier better routines.

Think about giving your children a balanced diet, not just meat, not just vegetables.

Consider what you eat and what impact that will have on the children. At one point I became vegetarian, this difference affects the children's diet so they still had some meat.

The portion size is another aspect of eating to consider.

SLEEP (ROUTINE)

Sleep is an essential part of everyone's routine and an indispensable part of a healthy lifestyle. Studies have shown that kids who regularly get an adequate amount of sleep have improved attention, behaviour, learning, memory, and overall mental and physical health. Not getting enough sleep can lead to high blood pressure, obesity and even depression.

Can you reread that last statement please.

It is like a golden ticket or top trump that beats everything. Sleep can solve any of those, maybe all of those.

How much sleep do your children need:

Infants under 1 year: 12-16 hours

Children 1-2 years old: 11-14 hours

Children 3-5 years old: 10-13 hours

Children 6-12 years old: 9-12 hours

Teenagers 13-18 years old: 8-10 hours

How to get children to sleep.
Routines, oh dear, do I go on about routines, they are the key to falling asleep. Have definite rules including when to go to bed and when you can leave your room.

Dim the lights, no one can sleep when their main light is on. It does not matter if your children are scared of the dark, all that means is that you have the light on outside the room, a landing light or a smaller less powerful table light. If there is too much light, your children will not go to sleep.

Electric screens. All the scientific evidence says that looking at blue light wakes your brain up. Lots of phones and apps have lock out times.
A nice bath will relax you and make you feel tired.

Little fuss. The more fuss you make around bedtime, the more your children will wake up.

Limit food and sugary drinks.
CHOICES / CONSEQUENCES (ROUTINE)

Many people do not want to be responsible for the choices they make, and they often do not want to admit that their decisions have real life consequences. Try as you might, you cannot escape the consequences of your decisions, whether good or bad. Every choice carries a consequence.

This section is very much about the choices and consequences you make about your children, and helping them make the right choices for better consequences that I hope will come. From that, when your children are adults, they will then make their own better choices and so better consequences.

37

I am not telling you how to live or what to do. NO. I would not want you telling me what to do with my life so I am not about to tell you.

No matter what, your children are YOUR CHILDREN.

This book is about helping you and supporting you. It is about you making choices about the parts of the book you want to use and the parts of the book you do not want to use.

It is your choice. BUT if your children are behaving in a certain way or you are not happy with how they speak to you, what can you do to change that? What choices can you make to change those behaviours?

How your children are and how they behave is directly related to the choices you have made. Their behaviour or attitude is a consequence of the choices you have made. I am not saying you have made those choices because you want them to be how they are, I am not. But because you have made a hurried choice, or a not thinking straight choice there are consequences.

I have spent 25 years making good, then bad, then indifferent choices, you are in good company. But it is time to be reflective about your choices, be more analytical about them.

Will making those same choices over and over again, create a different consequence?

NO, it will not. You know it will not. So, make some different choices and see what happens.

HOUSE FOCUS (ROUTINE)

Your house is the place in which you will create a caring, secure and loving environment. This is the place where you and your children will spend most of their time together. Sometimes you are all going to get on and sometimes you are not going to get on. Yes, there are hundreds of external factors that affect your children and you on a daily basis.

You are doing a great job of this already but there is always room for improvement. Even here you can be 26% better than before.

Does everyone get on? Are there siblings that don't get on? Are there times in the day when you or your children are not in such a great mood?

Stop reading this chapter and get a piece of paper and a pen. Think about writing down any times or people that regularly get upset or annoyed or even angry?

I hope there are not any but there will be.

Firstly, you are not going to fix all of these issues straight away.

Pick two issues, and only two, that you can focus on the house and yourself and your children. Try and prioritise them or choose a bigger one and a smaller one.

Do not be worried about moving people around the house. My older two could be terrible when they were younger, annoying each other and causing a rumpus. They shared an upstairs area, so I moved one downstairs. They stop annoying each other so much.

Separate your children if you have too. There are plenty of times that children and parents can have time together and your house will have a number of rooms. I would set up different activities for different children in different rooms.

Everyone needs their space. I would allow my older children to find and have their own space.

All children will get annoyed with each other and aggressive and mardy. Be creative in taking those negative situations and behaviour out of their lives.

MUSIC (ROUTINE)

Children are cooing sweet musical sounds, toddlers are humming and making nonsense songs all through their play, and little ones repeat their favourite tunes or tap out rhythms on anything that makes sound. Music is a large part of adults' lives as well. We sing lullabies to our babies and we hum while cooking, we use songs to celebrate birthdays, holidays, and special events.

Enjoying music is unique to humans. Unlike food or sex, music is not necessary for our survival, but it is extremely rewarding and pleasurable. It taps into the same parts of the brain that pleasure from sex and food does.

Music can help set a mood within in your house. If you want a calm and relaxed environment, the music should be calm and relaxed. You don't have to direct them to the music or tell them what to feel, the music will just do the job. In the morning put more lively music on which is faster and louder and more upbeat.

Music helps in stimulating the part of the brain that is responsible for reading, maths, and emotional development. It has been proven that children who were exposed to music while growing up excelled better in academics than those who were not. It gives your children a chance to express themselves. Learning and mastering an instrument takes time and patience, that are great attitudes to understand. It can increase confidence and creativity.

Sing bedtimes stories to them before they go to sleep.

Make and play home-made instruments or buy mini instruments. Keep them stored away so your children are not making a terrible din all the time.

Allow your children to take lessons at school. My youngest son started to learn the drums, after about two years he tired of it but really enjoyed the experience.

Buy a Karaoke program for your home console or karaoke equipment that the whole family can get involved with and play. One of the best Christmas we had as a family was when I bought my oldest daughter a karaoke set.

Take time to notice how your children respond to music.
ATTUNE / REPAIRING (ROUTINE)

Attunement is a way of tuning into your children. It is a focus on connecting with them. It is developing and focusing on having a better way of understanding them and so supporting them and encouraging them.

A parent who is attuned to their children will respond appropriately in language and behaviours to that emotional state.

Aspects of attunement include empathy. Do you empathise with your children? Do you get upset if they get upset?

Knowledge of your children. I spent many years getting to know and understand my two older children and found that I came to know them better than their Mum or biological Dad. I did that because rather than assuming I knew them I actively spent time and effort getting to know them. I tried to start with a blank slate and not just accept them as they seemed to be. I would listen actively to what they were saying.

Mindfulness is important in developing and enhancing your connection to your children. It is important to pay attention to your children in a non-judgemental way.

I feel that all these aspects then reinforce intimacy, presence and cognitive understanding of your children.

Sometimes children break the rules and the close attachment you have begins to breakdown. Children feel pain, shame or guilt.

As parents we repair this shame or pain by being loving and by understanding that your child might not be able to apologise straight away. Sometimes it is important for you to apologise for not supporting the child or not explaining to the child clearly enough.

All of this helps us to support our children with their emotional pain when they have it.

Through our role modelling and repairing these feelings and emotions, we are giving our children a structure to base their own resilience and processing of pain and discomfort.

PLAY THEORY (PLAY)

Play is an important part of a child's early development. Playing helps young childrens' brains to develop and for their language and positive communication skills to mature.

Simple games of peek-a-boo, shaking a rattle or singing a song are much more important than just a way to pass the time. They teach young children about communication, develop their motor skills, help with problem-solving and had been proven to develop their reading and writing skills.

Something as easy as stacking and knocking over blocks allows toddlers to discover maths and science concepts, including shapes, gravity, balance and counting.

Make believe play is another important aspect of your child's play. Creating make believe friends, or taking on the roles of other people's jobs and their characters, or using objects in a make-believe way is really good. Sharing this play with their friends again adds a social element to their play.

These early childhood games are vital to laying the foundations for formal education. In most cases learning starts through parents or carers engaging with, playing with and responding to the child.

So, join in with their games or their make-believe scenario's. You can make suggestions about the play and encourage the play activities.
Let them lead the play. Let them take charge of you and the situation. Ask them what your character is like? Ask what they should be doing?

Encourage your children to talk about what they are doing. Ask them questions about what they are doing so that there is a lot of verbalisation when they are playing.

You will see your children play along-side other children. By playing in a similar way to them but parallel to where they are. As your children get older, try and help them make their play more complex.

Remember do not stay too long. Your children need to play on their own or to play with their friends. They should not get used to an adult always being there to support and enrich their play.

CARD GAMES (PLAY)

A pack of cards costs about £2.50 and can be bought from most supermarkets.

Cards are a great way to interact with your children and a great way for your children to interact with each other. It is interacting but with rules and clear boundaries. This makes interacting a lot easier for all children. It also teaches your children fairness, following rules, winning and losing and most of all it is great fun.

When I say interacting, I am talking about socialising, listening to what other people are saying, waiting for your turn, having something to talk about and asking the other person about your cards or your hand.

SPOONS. The best game ever. However, many people are playing you take out and use that many sets of cards from the pack? 4 people, take out aces, kings, queens and say 10s. Make sure there is one less spoon and arrange the spoons so everyone can easily reach a spoon. Mix the cards up and then deal them out. Each person takes it in turn to ask for cards, I have 3 aces, so I ask for one card, everyone swops one card, the next person has 2 kings they ask for 2 cards, everyone swops 2 cards. You keep going until somcone gets a set of 4. Then they grab a spoon. The last person to grab a spoon does a forfeit. You can feint to get the spoon. But if you touch a spoon and no one has 4 cards then you do a forfeit too.

JACK JACK. All the cards get dealt out. Turn your cards over so you cannot see them and start putting them down in order, one at a time in a shared pile. If you put down an ace the next person puts down 4 cards, a king, 3 cards, a queen, 2 cards and a jack, 1 card. If your last card wins the hand, you take the cards and start the process again. If one of the aforementioned cards are put down the next person has to put down the right number of cards. The person who has all the cards wins.

My sister has a pack of cards with her all the time. When they go for a meal and are waiting for their food, or after they have finished their food, the cards will come out and the family will play. They will be all talking and laughing and interacting with each other.

There are many many more games. Type into google card games for kids and see what happens.

SOCIAL MEDIA (PLAY)

The issue of social media for your children becomes harder and harder path to walk as the days go by. I include adults in this too, our reliance on social media is intense and rewarding and complicated and dangerous.

Younger Children. Younger children should not have too much exposure to social media, it is illegal for children under 13 to have accounts on Facebook or Instagram. Tablets and phones need to be taken away from the children an hour before they go to sleep.

Teenagers. Computer games need to be turned off an hour before they go to sleep. Sorry, I used to take the controller off my son, so he literally could not go back on it when I had gone to bed. Give him time to finish his go or to save where he is. Most games now allow you to save where you are in the game.

Talk it through with your children. Try and find some common ground. Discuss some of the theory about the dangers of social media. Agree some guidelines to follow that allow your children some freedom to use their phones or tablets, but still reduces their over commitment to social media and that doesn't affect their sleep or school work.

Most phones now have an app or some kind of filter that stops you using your phone after a certain time at night or stops you over using your device.

I would ask that you look through your children's phone, randomly every so often as well. This will not necessarily be very popular and will depend on how well you get on with your children and how much they trust you.

Trust is a big part of this situation. As with so many aspects of your children's lives, you just have to believe that they are going to do the right thing at the right time, because you have worked hard to turn them into good and respectable people. Another part of trust is when it all goes wrong for them. Do they feel they can talk to you about something they have done on social media? I hope the answer is 'yes', I hope you remind them that if they need to talk to you, then you will not 'judge' them and not 'have a go' at them and you will, just listen and help them. You can explain that social media is complicated and complex and that all you want to do is help. Do not 'bang on' about this but make them aware that you are there.

BOARD GAMES (PLAY)

When was the last time you played a board game? When was the last time you bought a board game?

What board games did you play when you were a kid?

Board games are like cards. A really great way for everyone to have some quality time, all interacting with each other.

Second hand shops are wonderful places to get board games from.

The amount of new board games is staggering. My daughter bought her children a board game where you have to stop the animal from doing a poo, (the poo is goo). Her children absolutely loved it and wanted to play it all the time.

Board games are wonderful for developing concentration and for enhancing social skills, like taking turns, listening to others, learning how to win, learning how to lose and develop fine motor skills, (fine motor skills are the smaller, more precise moves that enable your hands and fingers to be able to write clearly and cut out). They also increase problem-solving attitude, extend critical thinking ability and are really great fun for the whole family.

You get more complex games and more simple ones.

I had a friend who was a mental health nurse and she would go and support families and children with minor mental health issues. She would always have on hand a game called Pass the Pigs. Each person took it in turn to roll two pigs. You would score points on who would land until you stopped or rolled the pigs in such a way that meant you lost all your points. If my friend had had 500 sets of this game in the back of her car, she would have sold every single one of them.

We live in an era where everyone wants to be connected, wants the very best graphics and the biggest memory and the most experience electric toys and yet, family after family after family, child after child wanted to play this very simple board game.

Remember, if you are not very good at talking to your children, playing board games is a GREAT QUALITY TIME ACTIVITY.

The board game industry in the UK is worth 12 billion pounds a year.
KEEP THEM BUSY (PLAY)
This seems like a really mean thing to write. As always with my bold statements, this isn't meant as BE BUSY ALL THE TIME. Your children should not be exhausted and burnt out, come the end of the week.

You children lead very busy lives. School is a very intense and hectic place nowadays, where teachers talk about the pace of a lesson and are trying to get more and more learning opportunities into a normal working day.

Children's lives are a lot more sedate. Too much time is spent on computer screens or consoles. There is too little time for moving from one place to another either by walking or cycling. We have to take the car or the bus or the train.

Children naturally have loads and loads of energy, and need an opportunity to get rid of this energy. How often don't your children sleep because they aren't naturally tired?

This is about integrating into your child's week a number of activities, to keep your children busy.

Even with austerity, schools generally offer all kinds of after school clubs, from Art to Football to Computer Games clubs. Clubs are great for your children to socialise and meet new people and are generally cheap because they will be subsidised by the school. They are a safe place for your children have fun.

Local clubs, especially sports clubs are very popular and again give your children a chance to make friends, learn new skills and burn off some of their energy.

Physical based clubs like Swimming or Karate in particular are great ways to get fit, learn about their bodies, get rid of pent up feelings and learn discipline and rules.

Joining clubs and going to clubs is having to make a big commitment. Both financially and in terms of transport. It means you or your partner or both, having to taxi, one or more of your children backwards and forwards. If this doesn't fit into your life and very often it does not, do not worry.

GETTING A PET (PLAY)

Owning a pet is rewarding but consider that pet ownership is also a huge responsibility.

The benefits to you and your children are fantastic and include:

Pets give unconditional love.
A pet can teach a child that he does not have to take out his anger or fear on others.
A pet can teach empathy.
A pet can teach confidence and responsibility.
Animals can help socialise children and increase verbal skills.
Pets can be very therapeutic for children.

Pet ownership is a long-time commitment. You are going to own this pet, look after this pet, feed it, walk it, groom it and love it for a large number of years.

Pets are expensive, starting with vaccinations, flea treatments, pet insurance, a pen, cage, toys, maybe dog walkers and food. This will mount up, especially if your pet becomes ill or has a genetic disposition to certain health issues.

Having a pet means fitting it into your very busy lifestyle. Do you have time to walk your dog? What will your dog do all day while you're out? Do a lot of research. You need to consider the size of your pet, depending on the size of your house. What do they need? How do you keep them? Check to see if your family have allergies.

Pet training is an important part of owning your pet. This is another commitment in terms of time and cost.

Who will look after your pet? In my family this was the killer question.

Again, it is important that your children help, especially if that includes walking the dog, lots of quality time, and fresh air and exercise. However, any jobs that need doing, should be small and easy to complete.

No matter what pet you are going to bring home, make sure to treat them well. I can assure you that it is definitely worth it.

CAR JOURNEYS (PLAY)

Car journeys are a great time to interact with your children. Short car journeys are great for talking about life, or practising your children's spellings or timetables.

Long journeys need more preparation and planning. Comfy clothes are a must. Do not clutter your car up too much.

Do not take too many breaks. Get your children excited about where you are going.

Always carry treats. This goes without saying really. Something they can chew for longer periods of time.

Play games in the car. Look up games on google. Think of animals that begin with A, then B etc. I will count how many red cars we pass and you can count the yellow cars? I will count the Mini's and you can count the Audi's.

Lie about how far it is. As a rule of thumb under 50 miles is "almost there". How far dad? "Almost there." Over 50 miles then divide how long it will take to get there by four. An hour becomes 15 minutes. Keep the atmosphere between you and your partner amicable.

Tablets are great for long journeys. You can pre-set them with films or particular apps. Do not use them for the whole of the journey. You use tablets as a change of pace, maybe later on in the journey when everyone is getting a bit bored and stressed. Take a laptop. Again, it is not something that you want your children to rely on too much. Download some films on to the laptop. Make sure you have earphones or earbuds. Take it in turns for the children to use that.

Tell stories using your own children's names. There was once a beautiful princess named Jessica who lived in a far, far away land.

A good game to play is, 'Hold your breath', this is a good way to reduce the noise level on a journey.

Children will mirror adult frustrations. Buy a sat-nav. The last thing you really want to do is get lost, NOBODY wants you to get lost. Every smartphone has a sat-nav, so use it.

COOKING (PLAY)

Cooking is a lifelong skill. A skill that has to be nurtured and developed and practised.

It is another opportunity to have quality time with your children. My Mum used to do cooking with us on a Sunday afternoon, back in the day, probably because there was nothing else to do. I remember it being fun and getting a chance to lick the spoon of mixture if I had been good.

Be prepared. Have ingredients ready to go and all chopped up. No, do not get your children chopping things up too quickly. Knives and children very rarely go together. Make sure you do this together.

Concentrate on explaining what is happening, talk them through it, step by step.

Show them how to do it. Rehearse what they are going to do, do not just plonk it down in front of them or give them some complicated job to do.

Have many little jobs instead of one big job. Children get bored really quickly.

Give them easy jobs to do. Stirring is great and mixing too. If they do not like getting mixture on their hands, get them some plastic cooking gloves.

Remember to make them wash their hands at the beginning and then washing up all the utensils, which they like.

Do not try and rush it by fitting it in to a small time slot. It will always take longer than you think. Especially the tidying up part.

Make it fun. Do not worry too much the first time if you have not produced anything. Do not get too stressed if your kitchen looks as if a bomb dropped, it will look much better next time.

Do not just try and do it the one time, give it at least 4 or 5 times.

The next time you cook, ask your children if they remember what you did last time.

YOGA (PLAY)

Yoga is an ancient form of exercise that focuses on strength, flexibility and breathing to boost physical and mental wellbeing. The main components of yoga are posture (a series of movements designed to increase strength and flexibility) and breathing.

The literal meaning of the Sanskrit word Yoga is 'Yoke'. Yoga can therefore be defined as a means of uniting the individual spirit with the universal spirit of God.

There are more than 100 different types, or schools, of yoga, most sessions typically include breathing exercises, meditation, and assuming postures (sometimes called asana or poses) that stretch and flex various muscle groups.

Yoga might sound a hippy trippy idea for your children, but please do not ignore any idea just because you never did it. There is a lot of research that shows that yoga can decrease the secretion of cortisol, the primary stress hormone, which in turn can improve your overall health.

Have you tried yoga? Would it help you deal with your day?

The benefits of yoga also include better flexibility, strength and coordination. There is no competition when doing yoga. There is a definite focus on calmness and quietness. Meditation helps with mindfulness and mental health. You will learn control of your bodies. It will develop and enhance your breathing, thus helping you to breathe fully from the pit of your stomach to the top of your lungs. It gives children the chance to practice their concentration skills and help them think more clearly. All these benefits increase lifespan and slow the ageing process.

A recent study has shown that practising regular yoga and meditation results in higher serotonin levels (the happy hormone).

49

Many gyms now offer yoga classes but also there are virtual yoga sessions that can be followed at home. All you will need is a little space and some quiet. A yoga session can take as little time to complete as 15 minutes.

Yoga for you or your children or both. What a positive hobby for both of you to take up. No extra equipment is needed.

LIBRARIES (PLAY)

Most towns have a library. There will be one near you.

There is a delightful freedom to libraries. A safe place where your children can roam, without you worrying about them.

As a parent, you are establishing an example as a reader. By going to the library with your children when they are young, you can make sure they develop a sense that reading is a natural thing for people to do.

One of the most overlooked values of the library is that it provides resources for free. Of course, if you forget to return a book, there will be a price. Libraries are especially important during the summer months when keeping kids entertained with summer camps, family vacations, and other opportunities quickly eat into a family budget.

Opening a child's eyes to the many reading options available can change the way they approach books. To begin with, it probably comes as little surprise that children are more likely to read when they are able to select their own reading material. In addition, children often find similar books as they look for their preferred ones, meaning they are exposed to more reading material than just the one book in front of them at that particular moment.

One of the most classic reasons kids should go to the library is to receive help in finding materials. Though the freedom to choose their own books or other media is critical to developing consistent reading habits, having access to a knowledgeable professional who can help find materials on a variety of topics is key. Modern libraries are much more than just warehouses for physical copies. Connecting children with the library early teaches them that they have access to valuable resources beyond traditional paper pages. Users depend on local libraries for a wide assortment of educational, entertainment, and communication needs. In addition to conventional books, most media centres allow users online access, providing critical job searching and connection abilities for many citizens.

The importance of reading for kids has never been more apparent, and teaching kids to love reading is integral to any strong educational programme. Reading early develops strong habits that will very likely carry over to a lifetime of benefits.

SIBLINGS (PLAY)

The best part of a childhood is sharing it with someone, like your brothers or sisters.

Not every family decides upon more than one child. Recent research into single children, also known as singletons has suggested that singletons often have higher self-esteem, are more creative and independent, are more intelligent and more mature.

I think siblings are great. The proudest part of my life is that all my children love, respect and enjoy each other. They spend time together. They even have their own 'sibs' whatsapp group, that I am not on.

They can be independent to you. I don't think their relationship should be an extension of your own relationship. Why should it be? They are going to be their own person, with their own interests and passions. Children are not mini me's. Their relationships should evolve with their brothers and sisters and other family members independently. When my children stay with my mum and dad, their grandma and grandad, I have no idea what they are talking about or generally what they laugh about or enjoy together.

They should all be treated the same. This is the cornerstone of having more than one child. It is a law that has to be kept, whatever the instance or situation.

Children know when you are not being consistent with all of them. They can soon work out who is Dad's favourite and who is Mum's favourite. You have to spend the same amount of money on them at Christmas or birthdays and give them roughly the same amount of time and attention.

Yes, this is really hard but I feel that you have to do it.

Brothers do not always get on together. Sisters do not always get on either. You have to be the referee to any and all their squabbles.

You should support and reinforce positive relationships between your children. They should learn to be fair and consistent with each other because you are fair and consistent. Be patient. Make sure when one has upset the other, the one apologises to the other and visa versa. It will not always be easy but that shared experience I spoke about will help them bond further as they get older.

JIGSAWS (PLAY)

My Mum loved them and would have one on the go all the time. She loved the 'Escher' impossible pictures. I was never keen on jigsaws puzzles, until she started to ask me to help her.

Jigsaws puzzles are a wonderful, cheap and quiet way to entertain your children.

When you work on 500-piece puzzles, you are doing more than fitting pieces together. Jigsaw puzzles stimulate many different parts of the brain, making them beneficial for all manner of mental processes.

Being under too much stress in the long term can lead to serious health problems. Doing jigsaw puzzles focuses your mind on a basic task that requires concentration and reasoning. As you work, your mind moves away from the demands of the day. Your brain shifts into the alpha state, the same one you are in when you are dreaming, and you become calmer and more relaxed.

Puzzles are a perfect way to engage the whole family in an activity. Your family can find a whole collection of images that you like and spend time working on them together. As you put together each successive puzzle, both you and your kids will learn new skills and gain a sense of accomplishment upon completion.

Completing a jigsaw has a similar effect to meditation as it generates a sense of calmness and peace. Because our minds are focused, we find ourselves concentrating on the puzzle alone which empties our brains of the stresses and anxieties that we face every day.

Jigsaw puzzles are known for the addictive effect they have on those who try to complete them. Once you start, you simply cannot stop! The varying colours, shapes and sizes of the pieces hold the attention of even the most impatient of people.
Jigsaw puzzles are fantastic when improving fine motor skills which is why they are often completed by toddlers and young children. Yet this is still relevant for adults, as the small pieces require people to work carefully to slot the pieces together.
Jigsaw puzzles are hard to complete and the satisfaction one feels after slotting in the final piece of a frustrating jigsaw is second to none.

Completing a jigsaw requires persistence and is an important lesson for all ages.

SPECIAL NEEDS - GENERAL

There are a number of sections of my book that are very relevant to children with special needs. If your children are struggling at home or at school and you feel that this is related to something more than them not getting on with their teacher or them not liking the subjects being taught then the website that compliments this book can help you. i2eyeparentcoaching has a number of checklists that can guide you.

Unfortunately, any kind of special needs is a label, which can be good, my youngest son has dyslexia and because of that he had someone to read for him with his 'A' level papers. He probably did not need any help but it just gave him some extra help. The downside of this is students at the school and some members of your local community might want to then tease and humiliate your children. I am sorry if that sounds mean but that is what happens.

I feel that sometimes special needs labels then let the parent off any responsibility for their children. 'Oh, he has autism, there is nothing I can do about that" and they then let their children do whatever they want. Having worked in a special needs school for 15 years, I know that although those students have particular challenges, some of which are really taxing and vexing, that I never had a student who would not follow the rules or do what I was asking.

To be honest I had plenty of students who mainstream schooling had tried their best, but the special needs school I worked at, did certain things that the mainstream school, and quite often the parents of the special need's children did not do.

I am in no way, criticising any of those parents. They did and do an amazing job of looking after, nurturing and loving their children in a way that I do not think I could.

All children, all people are on a continuum, with all of them having certain traits, for instance, where do you park your car when you go shopping? If you park your car in a very similar place every time you go shopping, you are probably on the continuum towards autism. That's not to say you're actually autistic but you have some of those traits. The same for your children.

SPECIAL NEEDS - MY BOOK

Communication is a very important part of parenting any child. Children with special needs need to be spoken to in an uncomplicated way. Try not to speak too quickly or with too many words, or with too many ideas at one go. As I have said earlier, do not say 'Can you stop humming!", children with special needs will only hear the last word 'humming' and will probably hum more. Try and use the 7 second rule. Sometimes children's brains will not process what you are saying very quickly so say what you want to say, then in your head count to 7. By then they will have registered what you are saying.

Children with special needs are not very good at moving from one activity to another, or one place to another. Always give them a countdown of how long they have left doing an activity. " Ok, Tony, you have 5 minutes to go", then " You have 1 minute to go". If you have a sand-timer they are great for special needs children, and all children, in that they can see very clearly how much time they have left.

Plan your day. This is the key to having a happy special needs child. They need to know what is going on and when things are going to change, try not to surprise them. Do not randomly say "oh, we are going on holiday tomorrow, Mark". Especially for much bigger activities like a holiday, you will have told them 2 months ago and then be reminding them every so often, until the final week before and then every day.

Try not to be confrontational. Your manner, consistency and attitude will have a profound effect on your children. As long as the negative behaviour is minor, as long as you stop your child and make a point of explaining what they should be doing, instead of what they have done. They will learn not to do that. A child is running with a glass in their hand, stop the child calmly and explain that that is dangerous then ask them to walk with the glass. This has been proved to work better than if you shout at them or use "YOU"in sentences. "Why are YOU doing this?"

Try and distract them, when they become upset. Ignore low level negative behaviour.

Making a fuss of your child's behaviour is actually reinforcing that behaviour.

Use humour as much as you can. Special needs children love humour and love laughing and you being silly.

MULTI SENSORY (SPECIAL NEEDS)

Your five senses are touch, taste, sight, smell and hearing. Senses are very powerful and frame our reality. What we feel and think is based on what our senses are telling us. How often as an adult, have you smelt something or tasted something that reminds you of a past moment or feeling?

A multi-sensory learning approach is a term many schools use to describe teaching methods that involve the engaging of more than one sense at a time. This can involve the use of visual, auditory and kinaesthetic-tactile pathways but can also include smell and taste.

I mention schools not because you have now become a teacher, but because firstly it is a language or thought process your children will be aware of and be able to use. They will recognise and understand immediately so you will not have to spend time, letting them experience this. Secondly, if it works for schools, then why will it not work for you. I am trying to show you the best tools and strategies for communicating with your children and creating a similar, not an exact, but similar, caring and supportive environment.

Visual. Pictures of actions are a very simple way to use both visual and auditory senses. Planning your day, you can explain what you are doing and saying what you are doing at the same time. Next time you go into your child's classroom, you will see a similar set up. There are a number of apps and software packages that mean you can type out words and pictures will appear with it. You can cut out photos from magazines to represent the words you want your child to remember.

Kinaesthetic-tactile. Children with special needs often need some kind of fidget toy or multi-sensory toy. Stress ball, stretching thing, flashing light thing, stringy thing, soft thing, spinning thing, squeezing thing or bouncy thing are all great toys to use with special needs children. They are wonderful for calming, comforting and for distracting.

Auditory. This may mean playing music of a certain type or actually speaking like a robot or a monster.

Find little toys and fidget things that the children like, have a box of them that they do not have all the time but that you can get out if you need them.

AUTISM (SPECIAL NEEDS)

Autism Spectrum Disorder(ASD) is a term used to describe a number of symptoms and behaviours which affect the way in which a group of people understand and react to the world around them.

It is not a disease or an illness and cannot be 'cured'.

Approximately 1% of the population are on the Autism spectrum.

The symptoms and characteristics of Autism can range from mild to more extreme forms. There are certain core symptoms that adults and children have.

Communication. Children with autism will communicate in different ways to other children. They can have difficulty in understanding what is being said and why it is being said. They struggle with the language of others and the meaning. They quite often think in concrete ways and will take what is said in a literal way. "It is raining cats and dogs", will be very confusing to them.

Social Behaviour. Children and adults with autism find empathising with others very hard. This means that they will act awkwardly or inappropriately in social situations. They will not be able to play or read or understand social context very well. They will want to be solitary, and will be very happy being so.

Imagining and thinking. Children with autism have extremely good memory about their toys and what might have been said or done to them. They lack any kind of imagination. They find change incredibly stressful and will not manage any kind of change unless prepared for it. They tend to have very obscure and specialised interests.

As mentioned above, there are a number of strategies that will help your child and you deal with Autism more effectively. They will not mean really big changes, but much smaller and attainable changes. It will mean you reconsider your approach in a number of different ways.

Children with Autism, like all children, are funny, interesting, lovable, unpredictable; can learn and grow and can follow rules and understand and respect your family's ideals and aims. They will just need more support and thought and love.

A.D.H.D (SPECIAL NEEDS)

Attention Deficit Hyperactivity Disorder (ADHD) which makes an individual more likely to have short attention spans, be impulsive and hyperactive.

Symptoms of ADHD tend to be noticed at an early age and may become more noticeable when a child's circumstances change, such as when they start school. Most cases are diagnosed when children are 6 to 12 years old.

The symptoms of ADHD usually improve with age, but many adults who were diagnosed with this condition at a young age continue to experience problems.

Symptoms may include:

Hyperactivity / Impulsiveness. Children with ADHD will not sit still, will be constantly talking or fidgeting and will be unable to wait their turn. They will be constantly interrupting and acting without thought and will have little sense of danger.

Attentiveness. Children with ADHD will have a short attention span and will appear to constantly forget things. They will make careless mistakes and have difficulty organising tasks.

Looking after a child with ADHD can be challenging, but it is important to remember that they cannot help their behaviour.

-Some issues that may arise in day to day life include:
-Getting your child to sleep at night
-Getting ready to for school on time
-Listening to and carry out instructions
-Being organised
-Social occasions
-Shopping

Society is constantly becoming more self-aware and understanding of special needs like bipolar and autism through famous people talking more about their experiences both good and bad. With that greater acceptance and exposure, the people within our societies will change quicker but this is a slow process.

THE FUTURE

So, you're a 26% better parent. CONGRATULATIONS.

Your home life has slightly changed. There is more time for you and your children and that time is more focused. Your everyday life includes quality with your children. Everyone in the family feels more invested in, and definitely more validated, emotionally.

Your home life is more organised and consistent. Everyone knows what is happening this week, everyone knows what's happening today.

Your children understand and respect the rules and boundaries that you have in place. They find you fair and uniform in the way you deal with most behaviours.

The day follows a certain routine, which allows you and your children to have your own time but also that there are activities and time to share each other's time.

Your children still make mistakes, but with your support, they will make good decisions to right any wrongs and sort out any frustrating situations. They feel safe to explain to you how they are feeling and you in return will listen and value what they are saying.

You still make mistakes when dealing with your children. But now you are more analytical and will reconsider how that situation can be organised or resolved in a better way. There is a joy to bringing up your children. You feel very proud of what you and or your partner and your children have achieved.

You and your children are happier and more content. You are both well rounded and have a number of diverse interests. Your lives are busy and structured but not exhausting.

You feel more confident when dealing with your children both in a positive and negative way.

When it comes to parenting, little changes make the biggest impact. You already know how to be a good parent, no fancy app, or exclusive weekends or spending lots of money. All it needs is that you consider why what is happening is happening and take yourself out of the situation and can you do it a different way.

I hope this has helped you. Maybe not the whole book, but elements of book. If nothing else, you have given yourself the opportunity to reconsider and evaluate what kind of parent you are? I do not mind you sitting there and thinking about the stuff I have written is rubbish because you did it that way instead and it worked. I'm really glad that it worked for you, the fact that you have thought about is enough.

But maybe you have sat there and thought oh ok, I will give it a go. That's all you have to do, is give it a go. Try it and see. They say complete madness is repeating the same situation in the same way and expecting something different. That can be family life which sometimes becomes very insular. Who do you ask? Your friends, probably not, a bit embarrassing, probably. So, if I have helped break a particular cycle, GREAT.

I hope your confidence has risen. Not that you know how to deal with every situation that is coming your way, but that you feel confident that whatever happens, you know that you can fix it or change for the better.

I hope you feel happier and that you can enjoy your wonderful children that little bit more and I hope that your children really enjoy you much more now.

If you are not sure about the statements above, read them again.

Good luck.

i2eyeparentcoaching.com.

I have a website that I have been developing over the last 5 years. Included are short 2/3-minute videos that explain more clearly some of the ideas discussed in this book. Each month 4 videos are added, sometimes there is a theme to the month and sometimes the videos are unrelated. There is a membership fee of £3.99 per month to look at and use all the videos.

There are many, many PDFs that you can download and then print out for free to help your children at home. These P.D.F's support many of the routine and play based pages you have just read.

There is a link to my YouTube channel which has over 40 stories that you can use to help your children fall asleep at night.

I hope this will help you. Please get in contact with me with any questions or queries.

Why not give it a try?

Acknowledgements

Sarah Walker. A shared experience of bringing all our children up. Learning and growing through every one of those days. Bouncy ideas and strategies of each other.

Annie & Johnnie Walker. It has to start somewhere! All of the nature and all of the nurture. You and my Dad have been wonderful role models and loving and supportive parents.

Lynne Hughes. Thank you for speed proof reading my book. After all these years, you are a great friend.

Alfie Windsor. Thank you, Alfie for creating a GREAT front cover. You are very talented guy.

About The Author

Andy Walker was born in Tamworth, England in 1969. He trained to be a teacher at Reading University. He has enjoyed success in this career, becoming a Head teacher at the age of 32.

Andy is a keen tennis player and has a mean volley.

He is married to Sarah and has four children and six grandchildren. He lives in Dorset, England.

You can find out more information about parenting at i2eyeparentcoaching.com or email Andy at

i2eye.parentcoaching@gmail.com.

Printed in Poland
by Amazon Fulfillment
Poland Sp. z o.o., Wrocław

61977191R00038